Beginners Guide To

APPLE iPAD PRO

A Comprehensive Beginners Guide to Master the iPad pro
Usage, Hidden Features, Handy Tips and Tricks and
Troubleshoot Common Problems

2020
EDITION

MICHAEL

JOSH

Copyright

Printed in the United States of America
© 2019 by Charles Smith

Churchgate Publishing House

USA | UK | Canada

Table of contents

Why This Guide?

To start with, congratulations on getting the new iPad Pro 2020. Apple company has been producing magnificent phones as far back their existence. Fast forward to this writing. This user guide is pointing at, the iPad Pro 2020, which is the latest iPad pro apple as of this writing. What makes this phone stand out among all is that it was built on upgraded hardware, which enhances its premium features and some hidden tricks and tips.

To get the best out of this device, this user guide will give you insights and help on how to go about handling the hidden features, numerous handy tips, and tricks of the iPad Pro 2020.

About the Author

Michael josh is a tech explorer with over 12 years of experience in the ICT sector. He developed himself with his advancement in the field of information communication technology, which facilitates his writing skills. His hobby is exploring new things and fixing problems in its most straightforward form has been his focus ever since. Michael obtained a Bachelor's and a Master's Degree in Computer Science and Information Communication Technology from New Jersey Institute of Technology Newark, NJ.

Chapter 1

The journey so far about iPad pro

TIM COOK released the iPad Pro on September 9, 2015. He called it the biggest news in iPad since iPad and showed off some of its exciting new features like the ability to run two apps side by side without any lagging or performance issues. It offers a digital stylus of the apple pencil, which allowed for an angle and pressure-sensitive drawing and the simple, sleek design for bigger and better iPad. This newly released was a step above the existing iPad in many ways, but a lot of people wondered why Apple decided to introduce a new line of iPads.

The introduction of an iPad pro module was curious for a lot of reasons. Apple introduced the Pro line to many of its products in the past including the mac pro, iMac Pro, MacBook pro

but these were all computers, and Apple had never introduced a mobile device with the pro suffix. Even the iPhone, which is reaching so much height of popularity in innovation, didn't have the distinction. So, while the iPad was favorable for some possible reasons. A big part of may have been the iPad was quickly becoming one of the most used professional tools for musicians, artists, entrepreneurs, and more. Even more than computers. The lightweight design and touchscreens made them perfect for a pro user in all kinds of settings, and apple was picking up on that. Marketing the iPad as a platform for casual gaming, social networking, and media viewing was fine for a lot of people, but Pro marketing target Pro users' people who want or need a high-power device that can place them above the competition. Apple also seems to recognize that people who want Pro devices would be paying more for them.

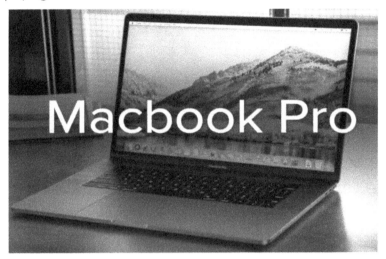

When the first iPad was released in 2010, it cost $499. Now a standard 9.7-inch 128GB iPad with wireless connectivity costs $559 with several less expensive options with less storage or no wireless capability. Still, the 12.9-inch iPad pro with half as much storage and no wireless capability cost $300 more. For the higher standard options, prices can keep up to $1300. Nonetheless, many customers want to pay for the pro functionality and performance that comes with it.

But the iPhone and the iPad might not be able to get away with such a massive price hike.

The iPad has enough diverse uses that are gone over surprisingly well. And in fact, uses for the iPad simply one of the most significant contribution apples has made to the tech world in recent years because people started to notice there is a shift in apple's focus. They started moving away from personal computers and turn to portable, simple and sleek devices. Steve Jobs was once having jokes that apple's idea of computers will be nothing more than the screen and the power button, and this seems to be where the iPad is headed.

Apple now holds a very significant portion of market share for tablets, and the good chunk of the company's revenue comes from iPad sales. So, the sooner they move customers away from a notebook in desktop computers, the better.

So, with the priors to the iPad Pro represents the next step towards the post PC era by inaugurating high power performance into the end of the device.

The iPad Pro was in part of a responsible growing market for larger-screen iPhones. One of the most notable most significant features of the iPad Pro is its size, which is several inches larger than a standard. Like the iPhone 6, 6 plus, and 6s plus all hit the market, the main for large iPhone sold. Unfortunately, as Tim cook explained in an interview, he said, the iPhone could mobilize the sales of the iPad mini. So, because the larger phones were creating some competition with a small tablet, apple offered a simple solution with an even bigger tablet.

We know that the iPad Pro is a push to a new kind of computing, but how does this device stack up to computers or other iPad modules. As far as its existence, the first generation of iPad Pro was different anymore from the original iPad. It was 12.9-inch as supposed to the 9.7-inch for the standard module, and also for the multi-tasking function, the large users used to use multiple apps on the same screen.

It came in three colors, gold, silver, and space grey. Three storage options were available, 32GB, 128GB, and 256GB. The cost of the first-generation ranges from $799 for the 32GB WIFI only module to $1299 for 256GB WIFI plus cellular module.

Some of the technical features for the iPad pro were carried over from the standard iPad; this includes things like touch ID and the reno display, which are the slightly improved resolution on the new virtual display, but there are also a lot of new editions.

The first iPad pro featured A9X chip and apple M9 motion cool processor and the 2.26Ghz CPU. These features made it an even higher performer than the iPad air2 and one even above and beyond with the higher quality camera through the turn on flash or without no flash, in adaptive screen lighting color. It offered face detection technology as well as an accelerometer, gyroscope, magnetometer, light sensor, and barometer.

As soon as the iPad pros initial released, the 9.7-inch became available. Of all contain the same hardware, it wasn't considering the new generation update, this version offered an additional rose gold model, and it was about $200 cheaper compared to the 12.9-inch module. For most customers, the real improvements came from the accessories.

The pro was released alongside the smart keyboard and magnetically dock keyboard attachment with the kickstand that turns the device into virtually an open computer. It was a cool accessory, but the biggest news was the apple pencil. It was in stylus design and explicitly released for the first iPad pro. The lord for pressure and angle sensitive drawing and writing directly on the screen.

Today, the apple pencil is compatible with almost all iPad modules, but at a time, it was one of the most significant advantages of going pro.

The first generation of iPad Pro was pretty well **received**; critics enjoyed the higher processing power in the larger screen, and customers were not impressed by the new display color reduction.

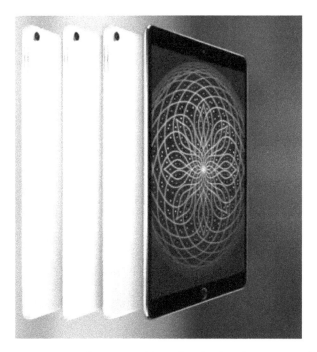

However, they were frustrated by the lack of power of the 9.7-inch module compare to its larger sibling. Apple responded to this criticism with the next generation released on June 5, 2017, at the worldwide developer's conference (WWDC). This generation did away with the 9.7-inch altogether and replaced it with the 10.7-inch module instead.

The second-generation iPad pro was the then-current generation to been sold today. Like the first generation, prices for the full-size 12.7-inch begin at $799 for the lowest storage WIFI only option and range another way $1229 for the highest storage WIFI inside the option.

For the 10.5-inch module, prices range from $649 for the lowest storage and WIFI only option and $1079 for the highest capacity WIFI plus cellular module.

Other prices of the iPad pro have stayed the same. Its storage doubled instead of 32GB, 128GB, and 256GB. The second-generation options include 64GB, 256GB, and 512GB, making the iPad pro the first apple portable device to offer 512GB storage capacity. Apple responds to critics about the smaller module having a 100 clock CPU. Both sizes now offered an improved 2.36Ghz octa-core apple fusion CPU as well as the upgraded apple A10X fusion chip and the apple M10 motion cool processor. As the first module, both sizes offered multitouch

11

through the turn on reading mode display and LCD backlighting and then internal reflective cooling. Also, both modules featured Pro motion, which equips the iPad pros to display with the 120Htz refresh rate. That means any quip movement on the screen like flicking through a webpage is notably smoother.

The cameras are also improved, and video recording was upgraded to 1080p

Finally, like the first, this generation of iPad pro includes face detection technology as well as the same ray of voluminous sensors, including the gyroscope and accelerometer barometer and amphibian light sensor, which works in tendon with through turn on the adaptive color display.

With all been said and done, the iPad Pro was a pretty high-power device. However, even after doubling its storage, critics start complaining the prices fall too high for a tablet device, especially considering most people who only need the power to stand on iPad for day to day tasks.

Many people seem to think that for most customers, the standard 2018 iPad is much better in cost and features options since it is now compatible with apple pencil contains 810 processor and offers up to 12 hours battery life.

So, most casual users don't know much about the difference between the two. But for those who need a high-end tool for business, music, art or graphics design the iPad pro is likely well with the premium price

The 2018 iPad pro was announced in Oct 2018, and it features a quite similar design to the iPhone X, a smaller bezel, and a larger display with rounded corners. It also equipped face ID, which only works in the vertical orientation. The famous headphone was nowhere to be found, just like the iPhone 7. As far as hardware goes, this version made some upgrade to its processor and chip with integrated Apple A12X Bionic (7nm) and Octa-core (4x2.5 GHz Vortex + 4x1.6 GHz Tempest). It came with no card slot, and it features different variants of internal storage such as 64GB/4GB RAM, 256GB/4GB RAM, 512GB/4GB RAM, and lastly, 1TB/6GB RAM.

When it comes to the display, it featured an IPS LCD capacitive touchscreen with 12.9 inches display and 85.4% screen-to-body ratio)

Now, the iPad Pro 2020 was announced on March 20. The 2020 version is slightly an upgrade to its predecessor. It featured a lightweight and two cameras with a LiDAR scanner.

Chapter 2

Setup your iPad pro

The iPad Pro just gets an exciting update. It is more potent as a high text center for AR. It works with the mouse and trackpad, and there is even a magic keyboard. The iPad Pro 2020 is officially the 4th generation of apple iPad pro following the announcement of its predecessors in 2015, 2017, 2018

iPad pro 2020

Silver, Space Gray   Silver, Space Gray

In the box, there are some usual suspects,

After the iPad is switched on, the very first thing to do is to swipe up, then you pick your language, and then you select your country.

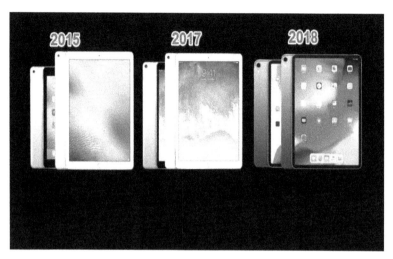

To set your iPad pro quickly, all you need to do is to bring the old iPad or iPhone next to it to get it setup. As you bring the old device closer, a prompt will come upon the old device and if it doesn't come up make sure it is running iOS 11 or later and it has its Bluetooth turned on.

 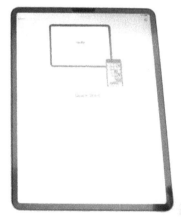

On the prompted command, the press continues, and your new device will automatically request to scan. Hold up your old device to the camera, then scan your new device. Input the password on the old device to complete the setup.

Then, you can set up your face ID, or you check CHAPTER to do that from the phone settings.

To set your new iPad manually, all you have to do is to tap on "set manually" then you follow the prompts that follow till you complete the setup.

Insert sim card in LTE version

If you have the LTE version, at the bottom right is the location for the sim port. Go ahead and grab your sim ejector, insert the sim ejector in the hole, then press a little bit for the sim tray to pops out, remove the sim tray out entirely with your fingers support.

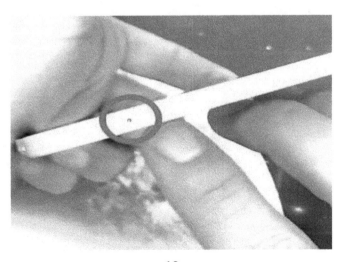

Grab your sim card, place your sim card in the sim tray, make sure the slit at the diagonal right-hand corner fits inside the sim tray slit, then propel a little bit to be firm. Make sure the hole beside the sim port and the hole on the sim tray are in the same direction, then gently slide in the sim tray with sim inside, and the sim id going to be installed.

Chapter 3

iPad Pro 2020 hardware

The new iPad Pro 2020 comes in two sizes, 11-inch and 12.9-inch. Both modules are identical every way except for the size of the screen, the weight, and the battery size.

iPad pro 2020

Silver, Space Gray   Silver, Space Gray

Comparing to the iPad Pro 2018 model precisely, the dimensions are the same except for the weight that has increased by about 10 grams for the 12.9-inch module and less than 5 grams for the 11-inch module. The screen is an LCD IPS display 264 pixels per inch (ppi) resolution. So, 2732 by 2048 on the 12.9-inch module. It has 120Hz refresh rate apple calls it Pro motion and couples of 100% DCI-P3 color gamut. It also has an ant eye reflective coding with apple claiming 1.8% reflectivity, and it can handle 600 nits of brightness. All of these are identical to the 2018 iPad pro, by the way.

Also, the iPad Pro doesn't have the fingerprint resistance recording on them, but well, I don't think I have ever seen this much free iPad screen. Corners around the screen are small when comparing to all of the other non-iPad Pro modules is that the edges are rounded in the self-square.

Just like on the 16-inch MacBook pro-2019, it has five studio microphones built-in so that you can use your device for on cam beat. When you look around the device on the left, there is a microphone, a few of their numerous magnets located around the device.

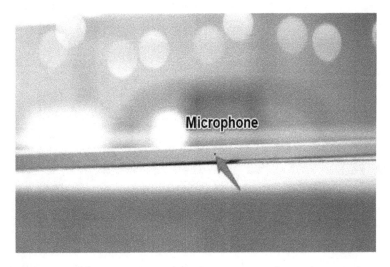

These are used for connected accessories such as the apple smart keyboard, for example. On the right, we have the volume up and down keys and a magnetic connector to attach the apple pencil tool.

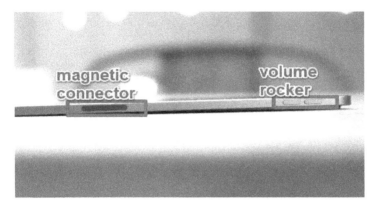

The pencil can be store there, but it also uses this to pair the device as well as get charged by there. Also, on the side, there would be a nano sim card tray if it's the LTE module. On the top, you have the three microphones used to record an audio and noise cancellation.

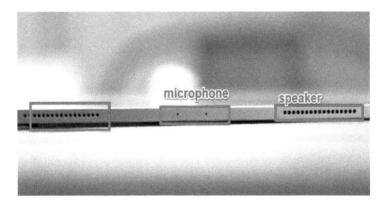

You have the top button that is used to bring up Siri. You can also say "Hey, Siri" as well for the screen to come one. Also, on the device, you have two microphones and four speakers. Two on the device and another two at the bottom together. A USB-type C port that can be used to charge the 36.71Wh battery on inside the 12.9-inch module and 28.65Wh in the 11-inch module by the way.

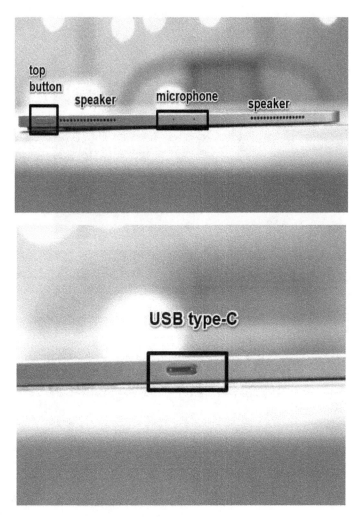

There is a new A12Z bionic, which is much more potent than the one on the 2018 model. The A12Z bionic on the 2020 iPad pro outscored the A12X bionic on 2018 in both CPU and GPU tests. The previous iPad pro was already pretty powerful so much so that it could handle tasks like 4k video editing.

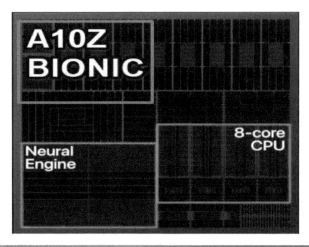

Not forgetting the WIFI 6, it hasn't essential as today, but it would be in the future when you are buying iPad pro you likely want it to last for several years. WIFI 6 even helps in number lead, including in congested areas, which is going to connect a lot of battery and take a lot less to one battery life. You can have better battery life in general because it has a new way.

Chapter 4

iPad pro 2020 camera

Above to the left, depending on how you are using it. There is a 7-megapixel camera then has an f/2.2 aperture. The cameras also pair with dot projector to project dot on the face and make use of the map and infrared camera to read those dots and a flood illuminated to add more infrared light if needed. This also the same setup as the last iPad pro (2018). The so setup, of course, it does allow for the well-praised face ID that works for sign-in into the device as well as to use it on safari to input your login details on a website, download apps from the app store, etc.

On the back, there are sets of new cameras with the second real camera in the 2020 model. First, you have a 12-megapixel camera f/1.8 aperture camera that is the same as the iPad pro from 2018 and a sensor size of 1/3 of an inch and 1.22 micrometer, dual pixel.

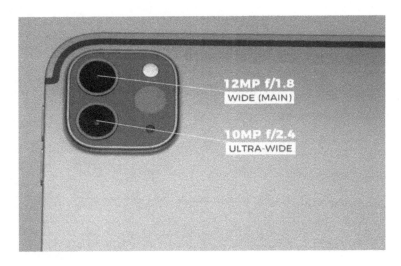

In addition to this model compare to the last iPad pros, there is 10-megapixel, f/2.4 aperture ultra-wide camera with a 125-degree field of view. But Apple sees the iPad Pro as a device for content creators aside from being able to edit the entire video on the lumofision app; apple wants the iPad pro also to be a device you can use for video capture. Both cameras shoot 4k videos.

Let's go through the camera modes and properties on the device

- ✓ **Panorama mode:** This lets you start to take a photo, and then primarily iPad has to stitch images together recorded in a wider panorama shot.
- ✓ **Square mode:** This majorly crops your images by one by one square
- ✓ **Portrait mode:** It only works on the front camera for some reason, but this one allows you to enhance the shallow depth to feel look.
- ✓ **Slow-motion:** This allows you to record video in 1080p and about 120fps (frames per second) to playback at 4x slow motion or 1080p at 240fps (frames per second) to playback at 8x slow motion.
- ✓ **Time-lapse (looped) mode:** This allows you to record video and automatically playback speed up.

✓ **Ultra-wide-angle lens:** The ultra-wide-angle camera also comes in handy when you are scanning the document with the iPad. It works in conjunction with the LiDAR scanner that built into the device. I will discuss more details on the LiDAR scanner in the next chapter.

How to change video quality

The iPad Pro 2020 can record video in high quality such as 4k at 24 fps, 4k at 30 fps, and 4k

At 60 fps and there is a way you can modify it. For you to change the video resolution, go to settings, tap on camera then record video. From here is where you choose the resolution and the fps of your video, and when you go back to your camera, you will see the option you selected above the screen.

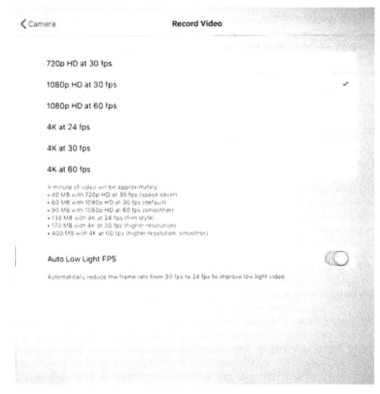

On slow motion, it can only record 1080p HD at 120 fps and 1080p HD at 240 fps.

Chapter 3

Set up apple pay on your iPad

Apple pay is a secure mobile payment and digital wallet service that uses or allow users to pay for things in physical store, on apps on your iPad or even on the web. Though, the web payment is limited to on the safari browser.

Apple pay is more secure than using the physical card. The reason for this is that for every time you use the apple pay, it uses a device specific number meaning your iPad uses the number it has generated and a unique transaction code to make sure you can type back to that particular device.

To set up the apple pay is quite easy all you need is to pay attention to the following steps;

How to add a card to Apple pay

✓ From the home screen, lunch the wallet app

Chapter 5

The LiDAR scanner

LiDAR stands for **light detection and ranging**. This technology works by sending beams of light that goes around it.

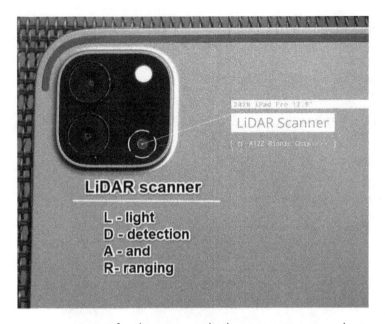

2020 iPad Pro 12.9"

LiDAR Scanner

[D - A12Z Bionic Chip ...]

LiDAR scanner

L - light
D - detection
A - and
R - ranging

Creating a map of objects and the space around you by measuring the time it takes for the light to bounce back. The new LiDAR scanner is meant to elevate the augmented reality experience on the device in which apple is commended to making a reality. One good example of this is the upcoming AR game called **lava**. This game will allow your phone to detect the object in a room accurately. It does away that in-game elements can inactivate them, including humans in the scene.

And there are scientific applications like complete Anatomy that uses LiDAR to measure the range of motion of some mount arm in the real-time.

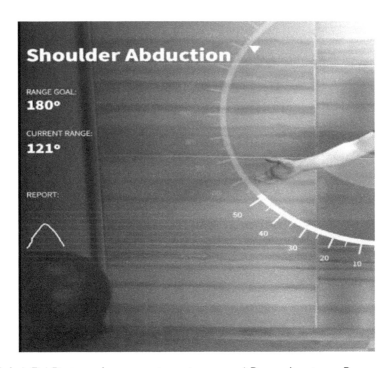

Shoulder Abduction ▼

RANGE GOAL:
180°

CURRENT RANGE:
121°

REPORT:

With LiDAR, it is also easy to set up an AR application. Previously, you needed to scan your surroundings by moving your device around. Now, all you need is to launch the AR app to start.

Chapter 6

How to connect external accessories

How to connect external trackpad

If you have a trackpad, you get even more features and exclusive gestures. The external trackpad can be connected to the iPad to avoid using the screen touch often. All you have to do is;

➢ Turn on the trackpad
➢ Go to iPad Bluetooth settings
➢ Turn on your Bluetooth
➢ Pair for a new device
➢ Tap on the trackpad Bluetooth name to connect.

Now, you can connect the whole iPad with your fingers.

Tips:

➢ Three fingers swipe up on the trackpad to go back home
➢ Three fingers swipe and hold on the trackpad to view the recent apps

- ➤ Three fingers swipe to the left and right to switch between running apps or webpages on safari
- ➤ To increase pointer speed, enable/disable natural click, enable/disable tap to click, or two fingers secondary click. Go to settings, general, trackpad
- ➤ Go to settings under accessibility to enable or disable the following options;
    - o Increase in contrast
    - o Automatically hide pointer
    - o Color
    - o Pointer size
    - o Pointer animations
    - o Trackpad inertia
    - o Scrolling speed

Expand port selection and storage

Another thing you can do is to expand your storage and your port selection. Since the iPad featured a USB type-C expanding your storage and port selection is simple.

Twelve South StayGo

If you have the twelve south stayGo dock (USB-C Hub for type-C) as everything you can need, including USB-A port, micro SD and SD card slot, ethernet, USB-C passthrough and has a USB-C cable integrated into the unit.

How to connect the external hard drive

You can hook up an external hard drive to your iPad pro itself and be able to transfer files back and forth from the hard drive to the iPad and vice vasa. This is super useful if you have a lot of documents to back up. Follow the steps below to connect your hard drive.

➢ Connect the hard drive to your iPad with a USB cable

➢ Tap on the authentication pop-up to grant the hard drive

➢ Open your file manager to access the hard drive

Connect game controller

Talking about things to hook up, you should also hook up the game controller to your iPad pro. Nowadays, many games are most exciting and smooth with the aid of the game controller.

➢ Go to settings and turn on the Bluetooth of the iPad

➢ To pair with the iPad, press the "share" button and the "ps4" logo at the same time until it shows the led indicator on the white interface

➢ Go back to the Bluetooth settings

➤ Locate the game controller name under available device

➤ Tap on it to connect with the game controller

You can play games like PUBG mobile, Fortnite, call of duty mobile, asphalt 9, real racing 3 and lots more. It is just a great way to play games on the iPad, especially if you have it place on the magic keyboard. You sit back and play just like you are playing on the console.

Connect USB Bluetooth mouse

With the release of the new iPad OS 13.4, which supports mouse and trackpad are helpful if you don't have the magic keyboard. All you need is an On the Go (OTG) cable that consists of the USB type A and C. The USB Bluetooth will fit in the provided port in type A while the type C will be plug-in to the charging port.

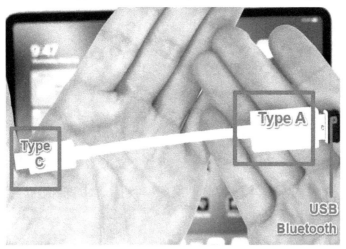

- ➤ Insert the USB Bluetooth into type A port
- ➤ Insert type C into charging port
- ➤ Turn on the iPad Bluetooth
- ➤ Turn on the mouse
- ➤ Search for the mouse name in the Bluetooth settings
- ➤ Locate the mouse name then tap on it to connect

Tips:

- The mouse cursor hovers on a specific app it is placed on
- Move the mouse cursor to the reference point below the screen to show the dock
- Keep on dragging down and pass the reference point to go back home
- Click on battery percentage at the top right corner to access control center
- Drag down on the left top corner to access notification center
- Go to settings, general, trackpad, and mouse to change the tracking speed, enable/ disable natural scrolling and select secondary click

Chapter 7

Device security

Enable or disable lock/unlock

The first settings you should change on your iPad pro or make sure it's turned on is found on the display and brightness settings. What this does when turned on is that it will make the device automatically lock when you put the cover, and it will automatically unlock when you take out the cover. So, if you have a case with a lid on your iPad, which most people do, make sure you have this enabled so you don't want per accident place the cover over your iPad and leave it unlocked. This will, of course, drain the battery.

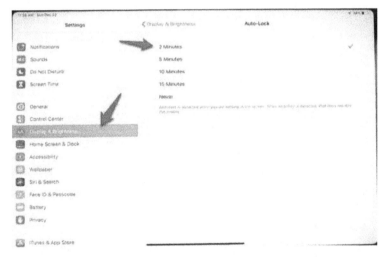

Under this same setting, you can turn on auto-lock on your iPad device. Just the lock/unlock, go ahead and tap on auto lock and you will find different options, choose whichever you want. I will suggest you select the minimum so, if you leave your device somewhere, it will be lock automatically under a short time.

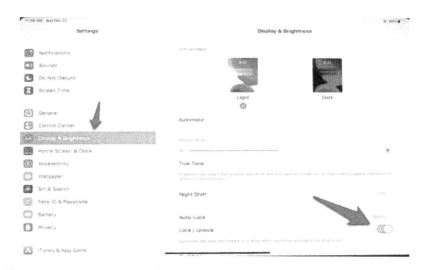

If you don't enable this feature, if you leave or forget your device somewhere, it would stay unlocked, and someone might get access to your device cheaply.

Activate face ID and passcode

The next setting you should consider on your new device is the ID and passcode enabling as these two are essential. The following are;

Require attention for face ID: this requires you to have full focus on your iPad in other for the iPad to unlock using face ID. Now, if you disable it, face ID would work a bit faster, but it is less secure than having it enabled. I suggest you always have this turn ON on your iPad.

Attention aware feature: This one is cool; it would add basically like a very cool feature to your iPad. If you enable this, then it would detect if you are looking at your iPad and that way it will be silent or lower the volume of notifications, the screen display will not go off. If you stop looking at your iPad, it knows and immediately dims your display in other to save battery. So, it is incredible, and of course, it would help your iPad battery performance in so many ways.

Allow access when locked: There are many actions under this section, which can be accessed from your phone when your device is lock. The steps are as follows;

➢ **Today view:** This is a handy and quick feature on your iPad that gives you information and an overview of some events of the day or appointments of the day, such as today's summary, traffic condition, calendar, reminders, stocks, etc.

➢ **Notification center:** This allows your notifications history from different apps on your iPad. It will enable you to scroll back and see what you have missed so far.

➢ **Control center:** This feature allows you to access some of your device settings from the home screen or lock screen.

➢ **Siri:** This is an apple virtual assistant that influenced getting things done faster and with a voice command.

All these can be accessed through your iPad even though you have it lock with a passcode or face ID. So, to make sure your device is more secure, I suggest you turn off all these features.

Chapter 8

Home screen & Swipe gesture controls

Going home & switching apps

Users may be wondering how to go back to the home screen without the home button with the device. With vast technology, the most device now uses gesture to navigate around on the phone. Going back home is quite very simple on the iPad. All you have to do is to swipe up quickly from the bottom of the screen.

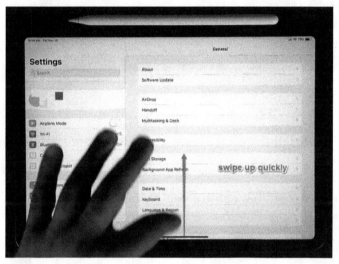

Also, switching between apps is very simple and impressive. If you do have many apps launched, you can switch between them only by swiping to the side of the bottom. Use the black small horizontal line as the reference point.

Access the control center

You can access the control center from the home screen or anywhere on the phone. Swipe down from the top right corner of the screen to access the control center. Swipe up to close it

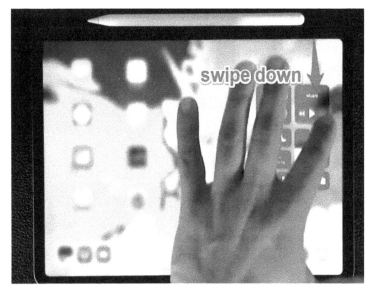

Access notification center/today screen

Just like the control center, today's screen can also be accessed anywhere on the screen. Swipe from the top-center to access it. Swipe up to leave screen today. Here is where you have all your notifications and any events reminder.

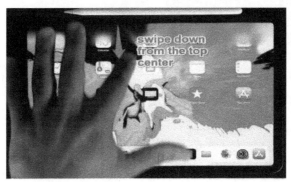

Swipe from bottom to unlock

Just like going back to the home screen, though, this is quite different as the phone will be on the lock screen to do the swiping. To unlock your iPad, swipe up from the bottom of the screen. If security is enabled, input it to complete the action, and if not, it will unlock straight away.

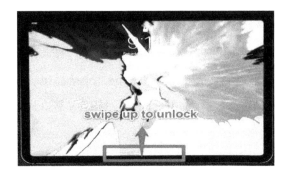

Access & edit dock apps

Over the years, the dock has always been rigid at the bottom of the home screen and not movable, but the apps there do. With iPad OS 13, Apple put an end to this, and it floats out ehn you only need it. Swipe up gently from the reference point to access the dock apps. You can also edit the apps on the dock. Press and hold any app on the dock, drag, and drop to the app vault. Press and hold any app on the vault, drag, and drop on the pier.

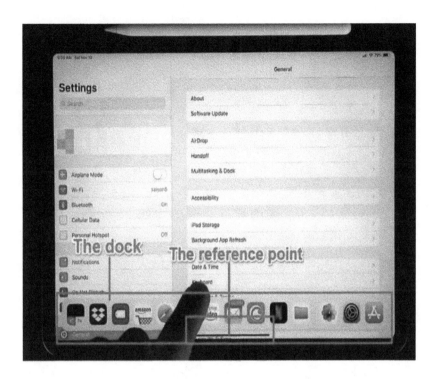

Access to recent apps

The recent apps can be accessed on the iPad with this simple idea.
Swipe and hold from the bottom of the screen to the middle, and
all recent apps will be displayed.

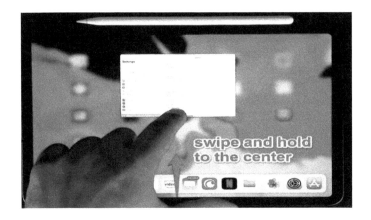

Pin widget to today's view

Your favorite widget(s) can be pin to the home screen to quickly access and control. To get this done, all you have to do is, swipe down from the left, tap on "edit" to have access to different widgets. Check "pin favorite" there are placeholders with the word "drag a widget here to pin." Now from the various widgets, press hold and drag your favorite apps to it until you are satisfied. Repeat this action several times until you have your choice number of apps to appear there. When you are through, tap "done" at the upper left corner.

Activate and customize home button

The home button is gone, but some people still want to have it. We can never tell if the reader of this guide will need it. So, there is a way actually to enable it.

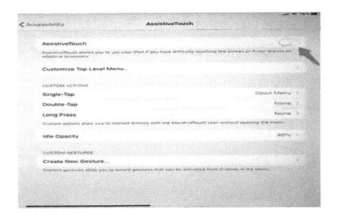

Go to the settings and scroll down to general, tap on it, then accessibility. Check for an assistive touch under the INTERACTION section then enable it. As soon as you do that, the home button will be displayed on the screen, but it is not going to function as the home button but multi-functional. To access the home function, tap on it to view other options then tap on the home button.

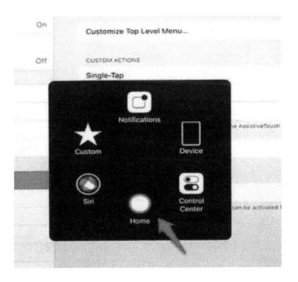

Apple made it easy; you can have the home button without any other functionality. Go to the settings and under the assistive touch, tap on customizing top-level menu, tap on the negative sign to remove everything, then tap on custom and pick home. Now it serves as the home button only.

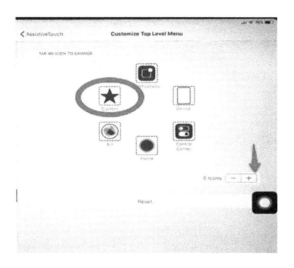

Customize the control center

The control center is what you are going to be accessing a lot, and for this, you can customize it to your satisfaction. All you have to do is go to setting, tap on the control center, then tap on customize controls and you can add or remove controls from the control center. Everything at the top with a negative sign red icon is included in the control center, and everything at the bottom with a negative sign green icon is the controls you can add to the control center. To add any of the options to the control center, go to the green icon beside any of the options you want to add and tap on it to add the choice automatically. Likewise, to remove an option from the control center, go to the red icon beside the option you want to remove then tap on it to remove the list automatically.

You can also change the position of the control center to your choice of interest. On the customize interface, there is a menu option (three small horizontal lines) in front of each option, hold the menu and move to the desire position within the removable option to change its position.

Additionally, you can expand each option from the control center for more options. All you have to do is press and hold on anyone to show its other functionality. For example, if you press and hold on a music player, you have three other different options.

Control center quick settings and their meaning

Airplane mode

 Airplane mode is mostly on all devices. It is turn on while on the plane to disable cellular, Bluetooth, and WIFI connection to avoid radio interference. Press and hold on it for more options

Cellular

 Cellular is a radio network distributed over land areas called **cells**. The cellular network also enables the phone to access voice calls and receive SMSs. When mobile data is enabled on the cellular, the iPad will be connected to the internet. Press and hold on it for more options.

Bluetooth

 Bluetooth connectivity is an aged technology on mobile devices. It aids connection between supported devices to transfer small files size, play music on another headphone, connect game controller, keyboard, mouse, etc. Press and hold on it for more options.

WIFI

 WIFI is a wireless connection that uses radio waves to access high-speed network connections and the internet. The term "WIFI" simply means "wireless fidelity." It can also be used in place of cellular network if one is out of its coverage. Press and hold on it for more options.

Easy access control

 This is a sub-control panel which gives room to control music player without the need to leave the control panel. Press and hold on it for more options.

Screen rotate lock

 This determines the screen display type you will have on your iPad the moment it is lock. If you disable it and you place your iPad horizontally, the screen will rotate. If that moment you tap on it to lock, the display will remain in landscape mode until you unlock and place the iPad vertically then lock to stay in portrait mode.

Do Not Disturb (DND)

DND puts an end to any form of sounds or vibration on the iPad if it is enabled. Be it alarm, incoming calls ring, SMS ring, video sounds, music, etc. This is very useful if you are in a gathering which doesn't allow any form of distraction. DND, while driving, is also an essential feature of this technology. If you are driving and DND mode is activated, it will automatically reply by text message to let anyone who calls be aware you're driving, and you will get back when you reach your destination.

Brightness

With this, you can increase and decrease the screen brightness by swiping up and down, respectively. Press and hold on it to give an option to turn ON/OFF "Night shift" and "True tone."

The true tone is a display feature that measures the ambient light color and sensor that adjust the background lightning around to relate with the iPad display.

Night shift uses the geopolitical and clock to automatically adjust the display in the screen to the warmer end of the spectrum after dark. The night shift option can be scheduled.

Volume control

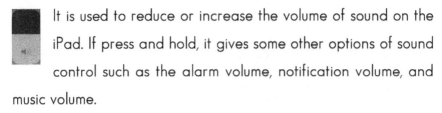 It is used to reduce or increase the volume of sound on the iPad. If press and hold, it gives some other options of sound control such as the alarm volume, notification volume, and music volume.

Low Power Mode

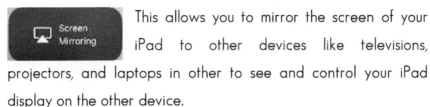 Lower power mode improves your iPad battery life by getting rid of less used apps that consumes part of the battery. The control center can fill up and edits with the remaining quick settings such as; timer⌾, accessibility shortcut, alarm⌾, voice memo, magnifier, etc.

Screen mirroring

This allows you to mirror the screen of your iPad to other devices like televisions, projectors, and laptops in other to see and control your iPad display on the other device.

Chapter 11

Handy tips & tricks

Ways and how to take a screenshot

There are two ways you can take a screenshot on your iPad Pro 2020 with ease and convenience. I will take you through the two methods as parts of the tricks in this guide. The very first one is taking a screenshot with the power button and the volume up button. Press the power button and the volume up button at the same time and quickly release it. The screenshot appears at the bottom left corner of the screen. Hold on the screenshot to give more options such as to share, add text markup, doddle, mosaic, and lot more. You can also swipe left to dismiss the shot or share and delete immediately in other not to litter your gallery.

However, if you have an apple pencil, you can also take a screenshot with it. Swipe from the bottom left-edge corner of the screen to snap screenshot as well. If you are on a web page or safari browser, you can snap the full page. After the screenshot, look at the top, "screen" and "full page" is there, tap on the full page to snap the whole page in a scrollable format.

Use QuickPath/floating window keyboard

With the floating window, you can quickly move around on the screen, the keyboard. It makes it convenient to type comfortably without stretching the fingers on the iPad. Also, space around can be used for some other things.

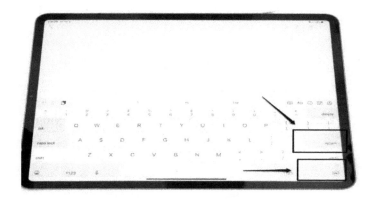

> ➤ Open an app that uses the keyboard (Note)
> ➤ Pinch in the keyboard with your thumb and index finger
> ➤ A small keyboard which you can move around will be formed on the screen
> ➤ Pinch out the keyboard to go back to full-screen mode

You can also press and hold on the keyboard logo at the bottom right and then tap **"floating."** Tap return for full-screen mode.

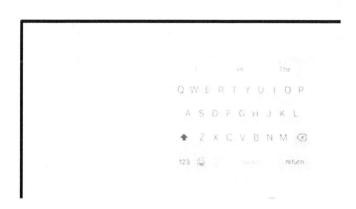

Use the keyboard as a trackpad

Instead of stressing the fingers to navigate the cursor in the right position, the keyboard can be used as a trackpad to control the cursor.

- ➤ Place and hold two fingers on the keyboard
- ➤ Move it back and forth to move the cursor

Copy and paste from iPhone to iPad

Over the years, people were worried about how to copy text and paste it on another device. Apple made it possible on their device. Texts can be copied and paste among apple devices.

The iPhone you are copying from and the iPad to receive it must be on the same iCloud account and be connected with Bluetooth and WIFI.

- ➤ Login both devices on the same iCloud account
- ➤ Connect both devices with Bluetooth and WIFI

> On the iPhone, select texts and copy it

> On the iPad, tap the space field to have the text then tap paste from the options given.

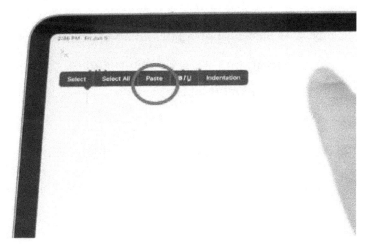

You can also do this in the reverse process. At the same time, it can be done on your mac if you are on the same iCloud account, connected to Bluetooth and WIFI

Handoff and its properties

Handoff is another feature you can do between devices as long as both devices are running the same iCloud account and connected to Bluetooth and WIFI. Handoff helps to mirror screen and transfer activities between apple devices such as iPhone, iPad, Mac, iPod touch, and Apple Watch. For example, you start reading an article on your iPhone safari but due to a small screen or you wish to continue the reading on your iPad.

Handoff requirements

Handoff works with the aid of Bluetooth Low Energy (BT LE) and WIFI, either directly or through iCloud. The requirements are as follow;

- A mobile device supported Bluetooth LE (iPhone 5 or later, iPad Pro (all versions), iPad 4 or later, iPad Air or later, iPad mini (all versions) iPad touch 5th generation or later, Apple watch (all versions).

Handoff apps compatibility

Apple had given the following handoff supports to the following apps;

- Keynote
- Numbers
- Pages
- Contacts

- Calendar
- Reminders
- Safari
- Maps
- Mail
- Some third-party apps

NOTE: *Apps are suggested to increase*

How to enable/disable handoff

Apple always enables handoff by default. The following steps will brush on how to turn on and off the handoff

- ➢ Open the Settings app from the home screen
- ➢ Tap general
- ➢ Tap handoff
- ➢ Swipe right to on

To disable handoff, repeat the same procedures and swipe left on the button.

Access Note app from the lock screen

The note application can be access while the screen is lock. It is now easier to access the note application on the go.

- ➢ Open settings
- ➢ Tap on note
- ➢ Go to lock screen and control center section

➢ Tap access note from the lock screen

➢ Couples of options are available. Such as;

  o Off

  o Always create a new note

  o Resume last note created on the lock screen

  o Resume last note viewed in the notes app

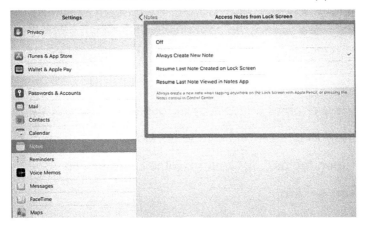

➢ Select any of the following except "off."

➢ To access this feature, use the Apple pen to tap the screen while it is lock

To disable this feature, go through the same procedures.

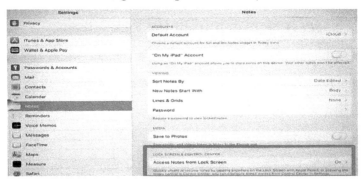

Keyboard shortcuts & their function

Different keyboards brands can work on the iPad. The keyboard features some handy keyboard shortcuts that will influence multi-tasking on the iPad—also, different apps with their shortcut due to the different functionality of each app.

To access these shortcuts, press and hold on the command key on the keyboard to display several key combinations for different actions.

Shortcut Key combination	Action
Note App Shortcuts	
Commnad key ⌘ + B	Bold
Commnad key ⌘ + i	Italics
Commnad key ⌘ + U	Underline
Commnad key ⌘ + shift + T	Title
Commnad key ⌘ + shift + H	Heading
Commnad key ⌘ + shift + J	Subheading
Commnad key ⌘ + shift + B	Body
Commnad key ⌘ + shift + M	Monospaced
Commnad key ⌘ + shift + L	Checklist
Commnad key ⌘ + shift + U	Mark as checked
Commnad key ⌘ + Option + T	Table
Commnad key ⌘ + F	Find Note
Commnad key ⌘ +]	Increase indentation
Commnad key ⌘ + Option + F	Note List Search

Commnad key ⌘ + N	New Note
Commnad key ⌘ + Return	End Editing
Home Screen Shortcuts	
Commnad key ⌘ + H	Go to Home Screen
Commnad key ⌘ + Space	Search
Commnad key ⌘ + tab	Switch App
Commnad key ⌘ +Option + D	Show Dock

Chapter 12

The Safari browser

Change download directory

With iOS13 and iPad iOS 13, of course, Apple has added a ton of new features to safari, like the ability to download files from safari. Now what you are suggested to do first is to update your iPad to iOS 13, then after go-ahead to settings, downloads, select the directory you want to download your files. You can choose iCloud storage or on my iPad for default storage. You can as well tap on other to customize your preferred directory from your iPad

Activate automatically close tabs

With the iPad, if the browser lags when you open it. With that, turn off your tabs that open in the background most of the time, we want them close one after the other.

So, what you can do here with the new feature of iPad is that you can set the tabs to close automatically after a day, a week, or after a month. To get this done, go to setting and tap on the safari browser, go to options under tabs, tap on the tab to select your preferred options.

Prevent ads from tracking your site

Another setting you should look after in your iPad pro is called prevent cross-site tracking. If this enabled, it would block ads from tracking your site from site to site. Sometimes you may be searching for a product or probably doing something online. When you get to another, you will see a bunch of ads, and of course, they are tracking users. You go ahead to settings, locate safari and tap on it and enable the feature under the privacy and security section.

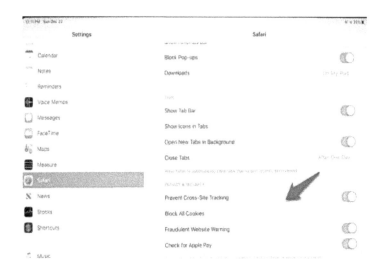

Chapter 13

Limit apps usage

If you go to the settings, scroll down to find the screen time option tap on it. If you are doing it for the first time, tap continues on the prompt pop-up.

This is going to manage the way you are using your iPad.

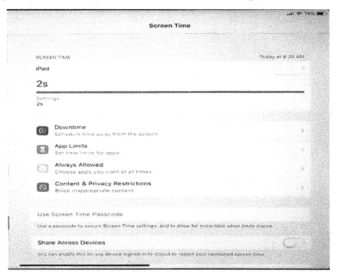

You can set a limit on your applications if, for example, you are playing too many games or watching too many movies. From this setting, you can set and manage how you use your applications.

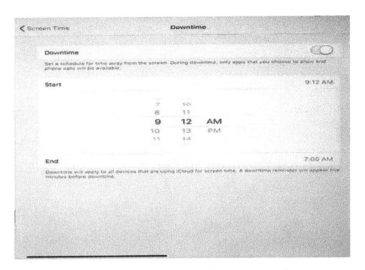

Now the first thing to do o the screen time option is to tap on downtime then enable it to set your preferred time the app will only be available for use. Tap on the back button, then tap on the app limit and add the apps to be limit.

You can set the limit time for each app you selected, or you select all apps to have the same limited time for all your applications. When you go back to the home screen, all the apps that you limit are blackout. If you launch any of the limited apps, it is going to say you have reached your limit on the application, but you can as well tap on ignore limit to access the application.

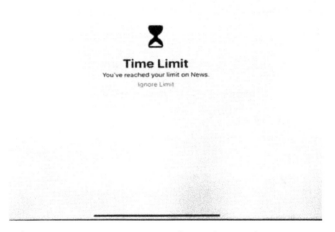

Time Limit
You've reached your limit on News.
Ignore Limit

You can also create an exception if you have downtimes enabled, such as don't disable messages, facetime, or maps.

Use screen time passcode

Screen time passcode will allow you only to have access to modify the downtime settings. It will make it secure as anyone that wants to access the downtime will have to input the passcode. The passcode doesn't make compulsory to be the same thing as the standard screen lock passcode.

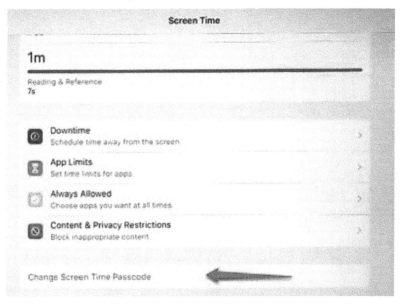

Chapter 14

Get started with accessibility features

Activate voice over on iPad

Voiceover goes through all of the menus and any text that is on the iPad, and it allows you to access those things without needing to read them. It is for people who have visual impairment who needs many using words read to them and be aware of where the menus are and can go through the iPad.

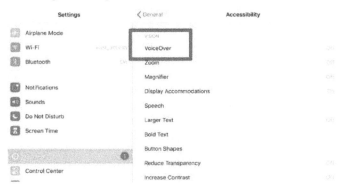

To enable this feature, go inside of settings and locate general then tap on accessibility. The voiceover is the first setting under vision. Tap on it and toggle or swipe right the button to enable it. A pop-up will surface with *"the way gestures work will change if you turn on VoiceOver. Tap each part of the pop-up to read it aloud. To continue, double-tap, "OK."*

The tone of the voice can be changed using the following settings blow on the page. You can also control the speed at which the VoiceOver reads using the **speaking rate** if you slide towards the tortoise logo, the reading speed slows.

The closer to the tortoise, the slower the speed but, the farther away, the faster the VoiceOver speed.

If you want to disable it, kindly go through the same procedures and toggle or slide the button left.

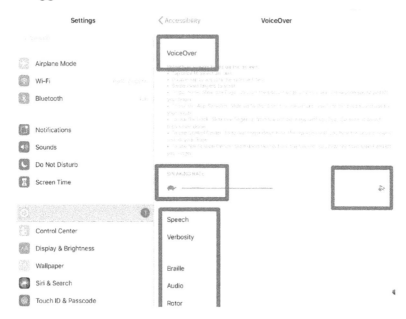

How to zoom screen for clear readability

Zoom is going to be very handy for kids to make a little bit extra help and zoom in the text, maybe with small myopia. Zoom is an accessibility feature that makes texts or anything on your iPad more significant for clear readability. To access this feature, go to settings, general, accessibility then tap on the zoom. If you turn the zoom on, you will notice there is a little bit square. At the same time, the zoom is enabled, double tap on the screen with three fingers to bring out the square again and drag the three fingers to pan around and move the square box to another region on the screen. Use one or two fingers to scroll on the particular section in the square.

Tap on the little bar on the opposite breath of the square to access other settings on zoom

- ➤ Zoom out: This gives options on the type of zoom to use. It's either the **window zoom** which is moveable around on the screen or the **full-screen zoom** where the zoom lens will cover the whole page at a time
- ➤ Choose a region: With this, you can change the position of the square (the zoom lens) to your desired area.
- ➤ Resize lens: Apple made it possible to be able to choose how to zoom you want the text. It is very useful and helpful as a teacher, as you can zoom out something specific you want the students to use
- ➤ Choose filter: this can help to filter the color on the screen to either;
  - o None
  - o Inverted
  - o Grayscale inverted
  - o Low light
- ➤ Show controller:

How to enable/disable follow focus and smart typing

"Follow focus" allows the zoom window to jump to the text been typed and follow it along. If the "follow focus" is enabled, you won't be able to in on the keyboard as you type. Unlike the other zoom options where the keyboard can be zoom. You can enable this in the settings under accessibility;

- ➤ Swipe right or toggle the "follow focus" switch. The green color is enabled while white or gray color is disabled
- ➤ Swipe right or toggle the smart typing switch, and the control will appear as follow focused enabled.

How to manage and use zoom keyboard shortcuts

Zoom settings also allow you to set up keyboard shortcuts to enables different zoom features while connected to an external keyboard. We are still under settings, general, accessibility and zoom

- ➤ Tap to open keyboard shortcuts
- ➤ Swipe right to enable it and other switches will follow
- ➤ Swipe the switches right or left to enable or disable the ability to use keyboard commands for;
  - o Adjust zoom level
  - o Toggle zoom
  - o Move zoom window
  - o Switch zoom region
  - o Temporarily toggle zoom

All the keyboard commands for these options will be displayed underneath it on the menu.

How to enable/disable the zoom controller

The zoom controller is a command that lets you access the zoom menu quickly zoom-in and pan around part of the screen and also zoom in and out.

Follow these steps to enable it;

> Tap on zoom controller, swipe right to activate zoom controller

> Tap on each option under controller actions to customize respectively;
>
> o Single-tap
>
> o Double-tap
>
> o Triple-tap

> The options under controller actions can only be assigned to the following commands;
>
> o None
>
> o Show menu
>
> o Zoom in/out
>
> o Speak on touch

NOTE: Two or the same command cannot be assigned to a single controller action.

> Tap back after you've assigned a command

> Swipe right the switch in front of adjusting the zoom level to allow slide on the zoom controller and double-tap to change the zoom level.

> Click color to select your desired color; you want the zoom controller. Either white, red, blue, yellow, green, or orange.

➢ Tap on idle capacity and drag on the slider to determine the level of opacity of the zoom controller while idle.

How to change zoom region

It is either you zoom in on the complete screen or within a moveable window screen. Don't forget we're still under settings, general, accessibility.

➢ Tap on the small bar in the square breath
➢ Tap zoom region
➢ Select full screen to zoom in the whole screen or select window zoom to zoom in within a window screen.

How to change zoom filter

Zoom filter allows you to select a preferred color such as grayscale, grayscale inverted, low-light, or None for the zoom region, and it would be applied to what is in the area.

➢ Tap on zoom filter and select from the colors listed above.

How to enable/disable magnifier

The accessibility features also include the magnifier settings, which allows users, most notably those with poor vision, to magnify their surroundings to be able to zoom in and out to see things vividly.

➢ Locate and tap the iPad settings on the menu

➢ Tap on general

➢ Tap on accessibility

➢ Locate magnifier then swipe right to enable

➢ When enabled, triple-tap on the home button to enable magnifier. It will show kind like a microscope that you can zoom in and see things. It is also helpful for students in the science department to zoom out to see words clearly on a paper.

zoom in

zoom out

You can also adjust the brightness and contrast base on the ambient light settings.

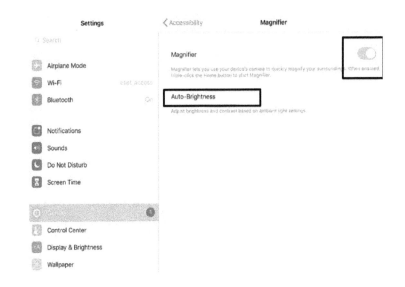

Chapter 15

Troubleshooting Common Problems on the iPad Pro

iPad won't turn on

If the iPad screen is faulty, it may be the cause of it to have a black screen while trying to turn on the device. That's why you may have the conscious the iPad is not turning on. To be guaranteed, if the iPad is ON, but the screen damage or the iPad isn't turning on at all. Make use of the apple "find my device" on another device to tell if the iPad is ON or it is OFF. Hardware damage like a battery connector can trigger it to occur. If the battery is also faulty, it can cause the problem that the iPad won't turn on.

To fix software related problems such as the iPad won't turn after iOS update. Follow the compiled solutions below.

First solution: Force restart your iPad

Many cases of iPad screen went black after an update is due to a software crash. It hinders the iPad from initiating a start-up and gets stuck on a black screen. Force restart could fix this problem and influence a power start-up.

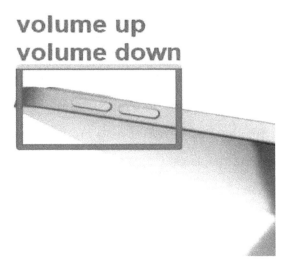

volume up
volume down

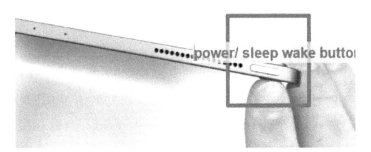

power/ sleep wake button

- ❖ Press and release the volume up power button quickly
- ❖ Press and release the volume down power button quickly
- ❖ Now, press and hold the power button until the Apple logo appears then release it

If the iPad has successfully turned on, allow the reboot process to complete, then updates your apps from the app store.

Follow these steps to updates your apps from the app store;

- ❖ Connect your iPad to a cellular or WIFI network
- ❖ Locate the app store from the home screen then tap to open it
- ❖ Tap today tab at the bottom
- ❖ Tap on the user profile icon on the top right corner of the screen
- ❖ Scroll down and locate the available updates
- ❖ To update individual apps, tap on update next to each app
- ❖ To update all apps simultaneously, tap on update all

If the apps updates are done, then you're good to go. Reboot your iPad for necessary changes to take effects.

Second solution: Master reset your iPad

Critical system error could surface after the system software update, which may cause severe threats like an iPad won't turn on. Getting rid of the current files on the iPad may help in fixing the problems s this will restore the entire system and remove severe glitches in the iPad OS. For Master reset to be carried out on the iPad, Mac, or Windows computer with the latest iTunes installed needed.

The following steps will guide you on how to master reset your iPad.

- ❖ Connect your iPad to your computer with apple supplied lightning or USB cable

- ❖ Press and release the volume quickly down button
- ❖ Press the sleep/wake button for a few seconds until the apple logo is display
- ❖ Open the iTunes on your computer
- ❖ Select sync from the iTunes main screen
- ❖ If a passcode is enabled on your iPad, input your device passcode to unlock. It will backup your iPad to the computer
- ❖ Click the option to restore iPad from the most recent backup
- ❖ Now, follow the rest of the on-screen prompts to complete the process

If you're successful with this, updates your apps from the app store.

Third solution: Recovery mode restore

If your iPad is still suffering from the black screen and won turn on, try and perform the recovery mode restore process. This method is a significant method that deals with different kinds of problems on iOS devices. Even if the bootloader is partially activated, it will still communicate with iTunes. A mac or windows system is required to carry out this operation.

- ❖ Connect your iPad to the system with Apple-supplied USBA/lightning cable
- ❖ Press and release the volume quickly down button

* ❖ Press and hold the sleep/wake button until recovery mode is display
* ❖ Select restore from the iTunes prompt options. It will allow iTunes to download software for your iPad. If the download takes more than 15 mins, the iPad will exit recovery mode. If such happens, repeat the steps to enter recovery mode again.
* ❖ Set up and update your device

Once the process is done, you can restore previous backups.

Fourth solution: DFU mode restore

If none of the previous methods can fix the problem iPad won't turn on, DFU mode restores, or Device Firmware Update has to be the last option. DFU mode restore is an advanced solution that deals with a critical system error and the highest you can go to restore iOS devices.

The important thing you will need to take note before you attempt this method is that make sure your device has no physical damage like accidental falling, which could lead to a permanently damaged iPad or a brick iPad.

* ❖ Using the Apple-supplied USB/Lightning cable, connect your iPad to the computer
* ❖ Press and release the volume up power button quickly

❖ Press and release the volume down power button quickly

❖ Now, press and hold the power button until the screen goes black

❖ After the screen goes black, press and hold volume down button while keep holding power/sleep-wake button

❖ Release the power/sleep-wake button after five seconds, but keep holding the volume down button until your iPad shows up in iTunes.

❖ Release the volume down button after your iPad appear in iTunes

❖ Follow the on-screen instructions to start restoring your iPad through iTunes

If, after all these solutions, the problem persists, kindly visit the nearest Apple service center in your area and have your device checked by their technician.

Not all iPad won't turn on are due to software-related. It can be a faulty hardware component on your iPad that coincidentally surface after software updates.

iPad Screen is Frozen

The following problems could be the cause of your iPad been freezing;

- Tablet boot-up issue
- Low battery charge
- Outdated OS or firmware
- Lack of space
- Faulty applications
- Memory bits or corrupted files
- Application conflicts

Having little idea of the likely causes behind your iPad could ease the chances of interrupting some system issues. Let's step on some possible solutions.

Free up space on your iPad

Sometimes, if there is no enough space on the hardware or in the cloud also causes the iPad system not to work correctly, leading to an iPad freeze. If you have access to your iPad, kindly free up space to avoid issues in the nearest future. To free up space, follow the below steps.

➢ Tap on settings

➢ Navigate to general

➢ Scroll down to "Storage & iCloud Usage."

➢ Delete unnecessary apps or clear nonuseful data from respective apps.

If you have enough space and the freezing still surface, keep your hope high and try out the next solution.

Avoid battery issue by charging the iPad

In some cases, if the iPad isn't well charging or not fully charge, it may appear frozen. Apple recommends charging the iPad for at least an hour. If the problem persists after you've changed your iPad, do not fret let's move on to the next potential fix

Reset your iPad settings

You might have tampered with a few settings on your iPad, which you couldn't remember where and how you got there. If you can still access your iPad, follow the steps below to reset all settings on your iPad.

❖ From the home screen, open settings

❖ Tap on General then scroll down to locate the reset

❖ Tap on reset then select "reset all settings" from the given options

❖ You will be asked to input your passcode

❖ Input your passcode to finalize the reset

One of the most effective ways to fix several issues with your iPad is by resetting the device. If this could still not fix the problem, do not worry. I have other options to get this problem fix.

Reset your iPad

While troubleshooting your frozen iPad, the first thing you have to do is to reset it calmly. This type of reset doesn't alter your iPad's data. You don't need to fret about losing any data just yet.

Soft reset

➢ Press and hold power/sleep-wake button until the slider appears on the screen

➢ Drag the slider from left to right to turn off your iPad

➢ If the iPad has completely turned off, press and hold power/sleep-wake button until it displays the apple logo

Force restart

➢ Press and release the volume up power button quickly

- ➤ Press and release the volume down power button quickly
- ➤ Now, press and hold the power button until the Apple logo appears then release it

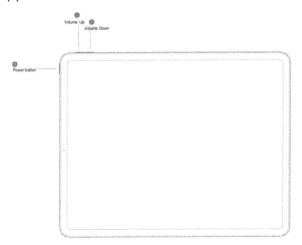

If any of the above reset options fix your iPad, let's move on to some other options explored before taking your device to an Apple service center.

Perform DFU mode on your iPad

If none of the previous methods can fix the problem iPad screen is frozen, DFU mode restores, or Device Firmware Update has to be the last option. DFU mode restore is an advanced solution that deals with a critical system error and the highest you can go to restore iOS devices.

The important thing you will need to take note before you attempt this method is that make sure your device has no physical damage like accidental falling, which could lead to a permanently damaged iPad or a brick iPad.

- ❖ Using the Apple-supplied USB/Lightning cable, connect your iPad to the computer
- ❖ Press and release the volume up power button quickly
- ❖ Press and release the volume down power button quickly
- ❖ Now, press and hold the power button until the screen goes black
- ❖ After the screen goes black, press and hold volume down button while keep holding power/sleep-wake button
- ❖ Release the power/sleep-wake button after five seconds, but keep holding the volume down button until your iPad shows up in iTunes.
- ❖ Release the volume down button after your iPad appear in iTunes
- ❖ Follow the on-screen instructions to start restoring your iPad through iTunes

If, after all these solutions, the problem persists, kindly visit the nearest Apple service center in your area and have your device checked by their technician.

Not all iPad won't turn on are due to software-related. It can be a faulty hardware component on your iPad that coincidentally surface after software updates.

iPad won't charge

One of the many issues being faced by iPad users is the charging problem. For the fact, your iPad has not been dropped on a solid surface or immersed in water mistakenly for an extended period, no reason for your iPad not to charge except for software related or firmware problems.

With all being said, here are things you should look into to fix your iPad won't charge.

- ❖ Connect your device with apple lightning USB
- ❖ Plug the apple lightning USB into a USB power adapter
- ❖ Plug the USB cable into a USB v2.0 or 3.0 port on a computer. Make sure the computer is on and not in sleep mode
- ❖ Plug-in the charger to the iPad charging port

If your charge successfully, a lightning logo will be observed beside the battery 🔋 logos. However, if nothing shows to indicate charging, then, here are the next thing you must do to fix this problem;

- ❖ Do a check on your iPad charging USB cable and power adapter if there is no sign of breakage, damage, or bent prongs.
- ❖ Use a power outlet and make sure the power adapter is fit in firmly
- ❖ Check and remove any debris from the charging port before plugging in the charging cable
- ❖ Plug-in your charger to your iPad and leave it for an hour. If your iPad still doesn't charge, then you need to force restart your device.

To force restart, check under **iPAD WON'T TURN.**

iPad won't rotate

iPad screen can be rotated from portrait to landscape to fit in the task being carried out on it at a particular time. This issue is mostly caused by software-related. Your iPad display won't rotate because the device orientation button is being locked or turn ON. A few approaches can be used to turn OFF the orientation key. The first approach is through the control center.

- ❖ Swipe down your iPad from the top right corner to access the control center

❖ Navigate and locate the orientation button

❖ Tap on the button to turn OFF device orientation lock

If the device orientation is turn OFF, and yet the problem still insists then, the device orientation app is crashed and has to be close by resetting all settings.

❖ From the home screen, open settings

❖ Tap on General then scroll down to locate the reset

❖ Tap on reset then select "reset all settings" from the given options

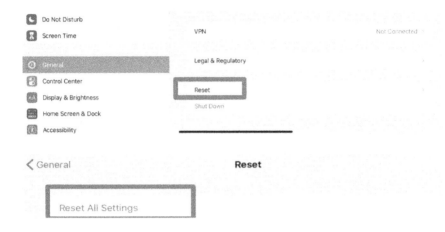

- ❖ You will be asked to input your passcode
- ❖ Input your passcode to finalize the reset

recover a stolen iPad

With iPad OS 13, you can find a stolen or lost iPad with the new feature Apple introduced called "find my device." If you can't find this app on your iPad, you can download it from the app store. If the Bluetooth of the stolen or lost iPad is turned ON, it matches its location through any nearby iOS device even if it is switched OFF. If, for example, a stolen iPad is taking to another location that's quite far or near to its previous location. During this course, if the stolen or lost iPad jam any Apple device, it will match its current location through the jammed Apple device. So, the person tracking the iPad will able to see its location on the map.

Friends or relatives stolen or lost iPad can be a trace on your iPad through your iCloud account. Don't forget to turn ON the "find my iPad feature."

- ❖ Go to settings
- ❖ Scroll down and navigate on "iCloud."
- ❖ Tap on it then locate "find my device" turn it ON

Now, follow these steps to recover stolen or lost iPad

- ❖ Visit iCloud.com on your PC or another device
- ❖ Login in your iCloud account

- ❖ Open "find my device/iPad" application

❖ Tap the drop-down "all device" at the center-up of the screen to access devices that are connected to the iCloud account

❖ Select the stolen or lost iPad from the list of devices displayed

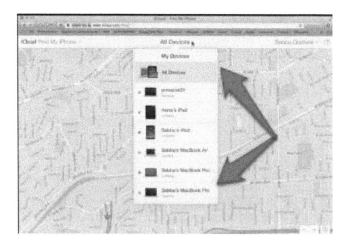

❖ The green color indicates the exact location of the lost or stolen device

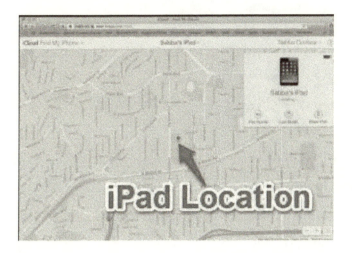

❖ Zoom in the map as much as you can to vividly see the device location

❖ If the iPad is misplaced within, click on the play sound button to activate sound on the device to locate it.

❖ If the stolen iPad cannot be located because it's not connected to the WIFI, tap on "lost mode" or make as lost to lock the device remotely. The lost mode will request for a number you can be reached. This number will be shown on the stolen or lost iPad. if no passcode set on the iPad before it got stolen or lost, you will be requested to input passcode to lock the device

Micheles iPadAir

3 minutes ago

Play Sound   Lost Mode   Erase iPad

❖ After inputting the phone number, tap on "next" to switch o message box where you will input the message that will be shown on the lost or stolen device. If you are through with the message, tap "done."

❖ Tap on "erase iPad" to erase your data on the lost/ stolen iPad to ensure no one has access to your wallet. If your data are backup, you can easily restore it on your new device if you sync it to your iCloud